To:

From:

THE 5 ESSENTIAL PRINCIPLES OF
THINK&
GROW
RICH

The Practical Steps to
TRANSFORMING YOUR DESIRES INTO RICHES

NAPOLEON HILL

Photo Credits
Internals: page iii, © PM Images/Getty Images; page iv, © PM Images/Getty Images; page viii, New York World-Telegram and the Sun Newspaper Photograph Collection, Library of Congress, LC-USZ62-136395; page x, Prints and Photographs Division, Library of Congress, LC-DIG-ggbain-13610; page xiii, Prints and Photographs Division, Library of Congress, LC-USZ62-78374; page xiii, © Keystone-France/Getty Images; page xvi, © PM Images/Getty Images; page 2, © Todd Diemer/Unsplash; page 4, Prints and Photographs Division, Library of Congress, LC-DIG-ds-10048; page 9, Thomas Edison Ediphone: Prints and Photographs Division, Library of Congress, LC-USZ62-55337; page 10, Prints and Photographs Division, Library of Congress, LC-USZ62-5515; page 12-13, Prints and Photographs Division, Library of Congress, LC-DIG-hec-06070; page 16, Prints and Photographs Division, Library of Congress, LC-USZ62-119898; page 18, © Evgeny Atamanenko/Shutterstock.com; page 21, © George Hodan/PublicDomainPictures.net; page 26, © dashu83/Freepik; page 28, © Lennart Tange used under Creative Commons; page 31, © ASISAK INTACHAI/Shutterstock.com; page 32, © jannoon028/Freepik; page 34, mrsiraphol/Freepix; page 36, © Petr Kratochvil/PublicDomainPictures.net; page 39, © Joe Ravi/Shutterstock.com; page 46, © jcomp/Freepik; page 52, © pathdoc/Shutterstock.com; page 62, © 2happy/stockvault; page 67, © Thomas Kelly/Unsplash; page 68, Prints and Photographs Division, Library of Congress, LC-USZ62-131044; page 72-73, Harris & Ewing Collection, Prints and Photographs Division, Library of Congress, LC-DIG-hec-24503; page 74, © Arthur Simoes/Shutterstock.com; page 77, © Ramiro Mendes/Unsplash; page 79, Prints and Photographs Division, Library of Congress, LC-USZ62-123429; page 84, © Jack Woodward/Unsplash; page 91, © Freepik; page 92, @ pressfoto/Freepik; page 95, @ Syda Productions/Shutterstock.com; page 108, Library of Congress Prints and Photographs Division, Library of Congress, LC-USZ62-136394

Published by Simple Truths, an imprint of Sourcebooks, Inc.
P.O. Box 4410, Naperville, Illinois 60567-4410
(630) 961-3900
Fax: (630) 961-2168
sourcebooks.com

Printed and bound in China.
OGP 10 9 8 7 6 5 4 3 2

Organized through 80+ Years of Research, Training & Unequivocal Results

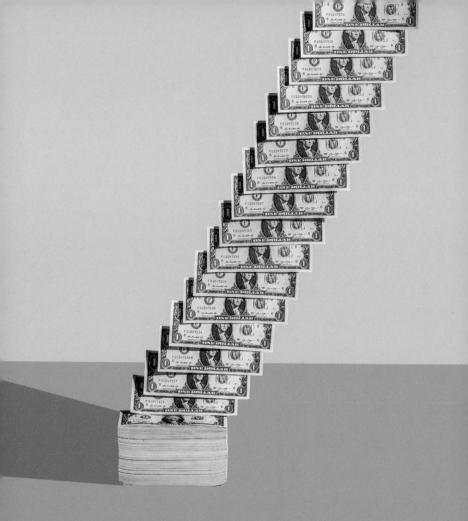

CONTENTS

PREFACE vii

FOREWORD xvii

CHAPTER ONE

Desire: The Starting Point of All Achievement 1

Desire Outwits Mother Nature 17

CHAPTER TWO

Imagination: The Workshop of the Mind 25

The Enchanted Kettle 29

What I Would Do If I Had a Million Dollars 35

CHAPTER THREE

Persistence: The Sustained Effort Necessary to

    Produce Success   **45**

    Symptoms of Lack of Persistence   **50**

    How to Develop Persistence   **55**

 CHAPTER FOUR

Power of the Master Mind: The Driving Force   **61**

    Gaining Power through the Master Mind   **66**

 CHAPTER FIVE

How to Outwit the Six Ghosts of Fear   **83**

    The Six Basic Fears   **85**

    Worry   **96**

    The Seventh Basic Evil   **98**

    How to Protect Yourself against

        Negative Influences   **99**

    Famous Alibis   **102**

ABOUT THE AUTHORS   **108**

PREFACE

IN 1937, JOURNALIST NAPOLEON HILL released the first *Think and Grow Rich*—a life-changing work based on his and Andrew Carnegie's belief that a fortune is within reach for all. To that end, Hill interviewed more than five hundred self-made millionaires with the goal of unlocking the formula to their success.

The trustees of the Napoleon Hill Foundation are pleased to present this special edition of excerpts from Napoleon Hill's classic book *Think and Grow Rich*. For this special edition, we elected to focus on the first word in the title: **THINK**. The book you are about to read emphasizes the many fascinating powers of the mind: its ability to desire and commit to a goal, to imagine

Napoleon Hill reading his original release of
the book *Think and Grow Rich* (1937).

the means to achieve the goal, to persist with determination to attain the goal, and to gain the support of the minds of others to achieve the goal.

For over twenty-five years, Hill was trusted to document and collaborate with the wealthiest and most successful businessmen of his time—resulting in *Think and Grow Rich*. This edition and all editions of *Think and Grow Rich* convey the experience of these men who began from scratch, with nothing to give in return for riches except **THOUGHTS**, **IDEAS**, and **ORGANIZED PLANS**.

Here you have the essence of the philosophy of moneymaking and other types of personal achievement, just as it was organized from the actual achievements of the most successful men of America during our formative economic years. It describes **WHAT TO DO** and also **HOW TO DO IT**!

For this special edition of *Think and Grow Rich*, the Napoleon Hill Foundation has focused on four important success principles: desire, imagination, persistence, and the Master Mind, as well as addressing the six

Andrew Carnegie, William Jennings Bryan, and others (circa 1910).

ghosts of fear in the concluding chapter of the book. The emphasis is on how the power of the mind can help you **THINK** and **GROW RICH**!

Napoleon Hill wrote that desire is the starting point of all achievement. And not just desire but a burning desire. Desire leads to the development of one's major definite purpose, without which success and happiness can never be attained. As a young reporter, Napoleon witnessed firsthand the Wright brothers' inaugural flight, surely the triumphal product of burning desire. He knew Thomas Edison, whose desire for the advancement of science and society was unmatched in his day and may still be unmatched today. Napoleon's desire to help his son, born without the means of hearing, produced a near miracle when after years of help from Napoleon, his son began to hear—to the shock of his doctors. All these examples of a burning desire are set forth in this book.

Napoleon said that imagination is the workshop of the mind. We all imagine. Sometimes that takes the form of daydreams, meditation, or artistic creation. In *Think and Grow Rich*, Napoleon emphasized how the imagination can be put to use to achieve financial success. Imagine in your mind's eye the many ways that imagination, coupled with desire, can lead to riches. This book can help you reach your goal.

The mind is amazing in its complexity. It has many facets and powers. One is its capacity for persistence. Persistence permits one to deal with failure, to recognize that it is only a temporary setback and can be overcome. Napoleon said that every adversity carries with it the seed of an equivalent advantage. That's a brilliant insight but one that relies on persistence for its fulfillment. In these excerpts from *Think and Grow Rich*, Napoleon sets forth how persistence can be developed and how the lack thereof can be recognized and overcome.

Napoleon Hill recognized that two minds are better than one and indeed that two minds in sync are better than two minds working independently, for when acting together in harmony toward a common

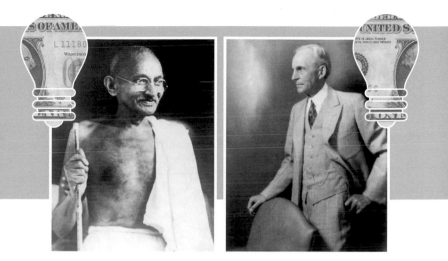

Mahatma Gandhi (circa 1940)   **Henry Ford (circa 1934)**

purpose, the minds become bigger than the sum of their parts. This is yet another fascinating truth about the power of the mind that is explained in *Think and Grow Rich*. Henry Ford and Mahatma Gandhi are two men who recognized and used the Master Mind principle to achieve virtually unimaginable goals, and their stories appear in this book.

Napoleon also recognized the power of the mind to overcome the debilitating effects of fear. His famous explanation of how to outwit the six ghosts of fear concludes this special edition, for it shows how the mind can not only achieve monetary success through the use of desire, imagination, persistence, and the Master Mind principle, but also produce lasting happiness and peace of mind by overcoming the fears that can plague all of us.

The Napoleon Hill Foundation is proud to present these profound and essential truths about the power of the mind that appear in *Think and Grow Rich*. Many people tell us that this is the most influential book they have ever read, aside perhaps from their scriptures. We hope you will agree and benefit from the timeless treasures in this magnificent book.

Don M. Green
Executive Director and Trustee
The Napoleon Hill Foundation

"If I had to recommend one book, it would have to be Napoleon Hill, *Think and Grow Rich.*"

—ROBERT HERJAVEC, *SHARK TANK* JUDGE AND TECH ENTREPRENEUR

INTRODUCTION

IN EVERY CHAPTER OF THIS book, mention has been made of the money-making secret which has made fortunes for more than five hundred exceedingly wealthy men whom I have carefully analyzed over a long period of years.

The secret was brought to my attention by Andrew Carnegie, more than a quarter of a century ago. The canny, lovable old Scotsman carelessly tossed it into my mind when I was but a boy. Then he sat back in his chair, with a merry twinkle in his eyes, and watched carefully to see if I had brains enough to understand the full significance of what he had said to me.

When he saw that I had grasped the idea, he asked

if I would be willing to spend twenty years or more preparing myself to take it to the world, to men and women who, without the secret, might go through life as failures. I said I would, and with Mr. Carnegie's cooperation, I have kept my promise.

This book contains the secret, after having been put to a practical test by thousands of people in almost every walk of life. It was Mr. Carnegie's idea that the magic formula, which gave him a stupendous fortune, ought to be placed within reach of people who do not have time to investigate how men make money, and it was his hope that I might test and demonstrate the soundness of the formula through the experience of men and women in every calling. He believed the formula should be taught in all public schools and colleges and expressed the opinion that if it were properly taught, it would so revolutionize the entire educational system that the time spent in school could be reduced to less than half.

As a final word of preparation, may I offer one

brief suggestion that may provide a clue by which the Carnegie secret may be recognized? It is this: *All achievement, all earned riches, have their beginning in an idea!* If you are ready for the secret, you already possess one half of it. Therefore, you will readily recognize the other half the moment it reaches your mind.

Napoleon Hill

Napoleon Hill

Author of *Think & Grow Rich* (1937)

Founder of the Napoleon Hill Foundation

1

DESIRE

ONE

The Starting Point of All Achievement

WHEN EDWIN C. BARNES CLIMBED down from the freight train in Orange, NJ, more than thirty years ago, he may have resembled a tramp, but his *thoughts* were those of a king!

As he made his way from the railroad tracks to Thomas A. Edison's office, his mind was at work. He saw himself *standing in Edison's presence*. He heard himself asking Mr. Edison for an opportunity to carry out the one consuming obsession of his life, a *burning desire* to become the business associate of the great inventor.

Barnes's desire was not a *hope*! It was not a *wish*! It was a keen, pulsating *desire*, which transcended everything else. It was *definite*.

Thomas Edison and his original
dynamo (circa 1906).

Five years passed before the chance he had been seeking made its appearance. During all those years, not one ray of hope, not one promise of attainment of his desire had been held out to him. To everyone except himself, he appeared only another cog in the Edison business wheel, but in his own mind, he was the partner of Edison every minute of the time, from the very day that he first went to work there.

When he went to Orange, he did not say to himself, "I will try to induce Edison to give me a job of some sort." He said, "I will see Edison and put him on notice that I have come to go into business with him."

He did not say, "I will work there for a few months, and if I get no encouragement, I will quit and get a job somewhere else." He did say, "I will start anywhere. I will do anything Edison tells me to do, but *before I am through*, I will be his associate."

He did not say, "I will keep my eyes open for another opportunity, in case I fail to get what I want in the Edison organization." He said, "There is but **ONE** thing in this world that I am determined to have, and that is a business association with Thomas A. Edison. I will burn all bridges behind me and stake my *entire future* on my ability to get what I want."

He left himself no possible way of retreat. He had to win or perish!

That is all there is to the Barnes story of success!

Every human being who reaches the age of understanding of the purpose of money wishes for it. *Wishing* will not bring riches. But *desiring* riches with a state of mind that becomes an obsession, then planning definite ways and means to acquire riches and backing those plans with persistence which *does not recognize failure* will bring riches.

The method by which *desire* for riches can be transmuted into its financial equivalent consists of six definite, practical steps:

FIRST. Fix in your mind the *exact* amount of money you desire. It is not sufficient merely to say, "I want plenty of money." Be definite as to the amount.

SECOND. Determine exactly what you intend to give in return for the money you desire. (There is no such reality as "something for nothing.")

THIRD. Establish a definite date when you intend to *possess* the money you desire.

FOURTH. Create a definite plan for carrying out your desire and begin *at once*, whether you are ready or not, to put this plan into *action*.

FIFTH. Write out a clear, concise statement of the amount of money you intend to acquire, name the time limit for its acquisition, state what you intend to give in return for the money, and describe clearly the plan through which you intend to accumulate it.

SIXTH. Read your written statement aloud, twice daily, once just before retiring at night and once after arising in the morning.

We who are in this race for riches should be encouraged to know that this changed world in which we live is demanding new ideas, new ways of doing things, new leaders, new inventions, new methods of teaching, new methods of marketing, new books, new literature, new features for media and movies. Behind all this demand for new and better things, there is one quality which one must possess to win, and that is **DEFINITENESS OF PURPOSE**—the knowledge of what one wants and a *burning desire* to possess it.

We who desire to accumulate riches should remember the real leaders of the world always have been men who harnessed and put into practical use the intangible, unseen forces of unborn opportunity and have converted those forces (or impulses of thought) into skyscrapers, cities, factories, airplanes, automobiles, and every form of convenience that makes life more pleasant.

Tolerance and an open mind are practical necessities of the dreamer of today. *Those who are afraid of new ideas are doomed before they start.* Never has

**Thomas Edison examining the Ediphone
with Edwin C. Barnes (circa 1921).**

The Wright brothers at the International Aviation Tournament (1910).

there been a time more favorable to pioneers than the present. True, there is no wild and woolly west to be conquered, as in the days of the covered wagon, but there is a vast business, financial, and industrial world to be remolded and redirected along new and better lines.

In planning to acquire your share of the riches, let no one influence you to scorn the dreamer. To win the big stakes in this changed world, you must catch the spirit of the great pioneers of the past, whose dreams have given to civilization all that it has of value, the spirit which serves as the lifeblood of our own country—your opportunity and mine to develop and market our talents.

The Wright brothers dreamed of a machine that would fly through the air. Now one may see evidence all over the world that they dreamed soundly.

The world has become accustomed to new discoveries. Nay, it has shown a willingness to reward the dreamer who gives the world a new idea.

Awake, arise, and assert yourself, you dreamers of the world. Your star is now in the ascendency. The world is filled with an abundance of **OPPORTUNITY** which the dreamers of the past never knew.

Wright brothers' plane flies over Fort Meyer
(circa 1909).

The greatest achievement was, at first, and for a time, a dream.

—JAMES ALLEN

The oak sleeps in the acorn. The bird waits in the egg, and in the highest vision of the soul, a waking angel stirs. Dreams are the seedlings of reality.

—JAMES ALLEN

Remember, too, that many who succeed in life get off to a bad start and pass through heartbreaking struggles before they "arrive." The turning point in the lives of those who succeed usually comes at the moment of some crisis through which they are introduced to their "other selves."

Edison, the world's greatest inventor and scientist, was a "tramp" telegraph operator. He failed innumerable times before he was driven, finally, to the discovery of the genius which slept within his brain.

Scottish poet Robert Burns was an illiterate country lad. He was cursed by poverty and grew up to be a drunkard in the bargain. The world was made better for him having lived, because he clothed beautiful thoughts in poetry and thereby plucked a thorn and planted a rose in its place.

Booker T. Washington was born in slavery, handicapped by race and color. Because he was tolerant, had an open mind at all times on all subjects, and was a **DREAMER**, he left his impress for good on an entire country.

Booker T. Washington (circa 1890).

Beethoven was deaf, Milton was blind, but their names will last as long as time endures, because they dreamed and translated their dreams into organized thought.

There is a difference between *wishing* for a thing and *being ready to receive it*. No one is *ready* for a thing until he believes he can acquire it. The state of mind must be belief, not mere hope or wish. Open-mindedness is essential for belief. Closed minds do not inspire faith, courage, and belief.

Desire Outwits Mother Nature

Many years before the birth of my son, I had written, "Our only limitations are those we set up in our own minds." For the first time, I wondered if that statement was true. Lying on the bed in front of me was a newly born child without any physical sign of ears, the natural equipment of hearing. Even though he might hear and speak, he was obviously disfigured for life.

What could I do about it? Somehow I would find a way to transplant into that child's mind my own *burning*

desire for ways and means of conveying sound to his brain without the aid of ears.

As soon as the child was old enough to cooperate, I would fill his mind so completely with a *burning desire* to hear that Nature would, by methods of her own, translate it into physical reality.

One day, I discovered that he could hear me quite clearly when I spoke with my lips touching his mastoid bone, or at the base of the brain. These discoveries placed in my possession the necessary media by which

I began to translate into reality my *burning desire* to help my son develop hearing and speech. By that time, he was making stabs at speaking certain words. The outlook was far from encouraging, but **DESIRE BACKED BY FAITH** knows no such word as impossible.

Having determined that he could hear the sound of my voice plainly, I began, immediately, to transfer to his mind the desire to hear and speak. I soon discovered that the child enjoyed bedtime stories, so I went to work, creating stories designed to develop in him self-reliance, imagination, and a *keen desire to hear and to be normal.*

The little deaf boy went through the grades, high school, and college without being able to hear his teachers, except when they shouted loudly at close range. He did not go to a school for the deaf. We would not permit him to learn the sign language. We were determined that he should live a normal life and associate with normal children, and we stood by that decision, although it cost us many heated debates with school officials.

While he was in high school, he tried an electrical hearing aid, but it was of no value to him due, we believed, to a condition that was disclosed when the child was six, when a doctor operated on one side of the boy's head and discovered that there was no sign of natural hearing equipment.

During his last week in college (eighteen years after the operation), something happened which marked the most important turning point of his life. Through what seemed to be mere chance, he came into possession of an electrical hearing device, which was sent to him on trial. He was slow about testing it, due to his disappointment with a similar device. Finally, he picked the instrument up and more or less carelessly placed it on his head, hooked up the battery, and lo! as if by a stroke of magic, his lifelong desire for normal hearing became a reality! For the first time in his life, he heard practically as well as any person with normal hearing.

Overjoyed because of the **CHANGED WORLD** which had been brought to him through his hearing device, he rushed to the telephone, called his mother, and heard her voice perfectly. The next day, he plainly heard the voices of his professors in class for the first time in his life! He heard the radio. He heard the talking pictures. For the first time in his life, he could converse freely with other people without the necessity of them having to speak loudly. Truly, he had come into possession of a changed world. We had refused to accept Nature's error, and by **PERSISTENT DESIRE**, we had induced Nature to correct that error through the only practical means available.

Whatever the mind can conceive and believe, it can achieve with positive mental attitude.

—NAPOLEON HILL

DESIRE AT WORK...

1. In your own life, what would you categorize as wishes as opposed to a burning desire?

2. Are you willing to pay the price that Edwin C. Barnes paid in order to make your wishes a reality?

3. What is the starting point for all achievement? How can you take your first steps TODAY?

4. Understanding there is no such thing as something coming from nothing, what would you be willing to sacrifice for your success?

5. If you know what you desire, do you have the belief in yourself to get the results you crave?

2

IMAGINATION

TWO

The Workshop of the Mind

THE IMAGINATION IS LITERALLY THE workshop wherein are fashioned all plans created by man. The impulse, the *desire*, is given shape, form, and **ACTION** through the aid of the imaginative faculty of the mind.

It has been said that man can create anything which he can imagine.

Man's only limitation, within reason, lies in his development and use of his imagination. He has not yet reached the apex of development in the use of his imaginative faculty. He has merely discovered that he has an imagination and has commenced to use it in a very elementary way.

The great leaders of business, industry, and finance,

and the great artists, musicians, poets, and writers became great because they developed the faculty of creative imagination.

Desire is only a thought, an impulse. It is nebulous and ephemeral. It is abstract and of no value until it has been transformed into its physical counterpart.

Ideas are the beginning points of all fortunes. *Ideas are products of the imagination.* Let us examine a few well-known ideas which have yielded huge fortunes with the hope that these illustrations will convey definite information concerning the method by which imagination may be used in accumulating riches.

The Enchanted Kettle

Fifty years ago, an old country doctor drove to town, hitched his horse, quietly slipped into a drugstore by the back door, and began "dickering" with the young drug clerk.

His mission was destined to yield great wealth to many people.

For more than an hour, behind the prescription counter, the old doctor and the clerk talked in low tones. Then the doctor left. He went out to the buggy and brought back a large, old-fashioned kettle and a big wooden paddle (used for stirring the contents of the kettle) and deposited them in the back of the store.

The clerk inspected the kettle, reached into his inside pocket, took out a roll of bills, and handed it over to the doctor. The roll contained exactly $500.00—the clerk's entire savings!

The doctor handed over a small slip of paper on which was written a secret formula. The words on that small slip of paper were worth a king's ransom! *But not to the doctor!* Those magic words were needed to start the kettle boiling, but neither the doctor nor the young clerk knew what fabulous fortunes were destined to flow from that kettle.

The old doctor was glad to sell the outfit for five hundred dollars. The money would pay off his debts and give him freedom of mind. The clerk was taking a big chance by staking his entire life's savings on a mere scrap of paper and an old kettle! He never dreamed his investment would start a kettle to overflowing with gold that would surpass the miraculous performance of Aladdin's lamp.

What the clerk *really purchased* was an **IDEA**!

The old kettle and the wooden paddle and the secret message on a slip of paper were incidental. The strange performance of that kettle began to take place after the new owner mixed with the secret instructions an ingredient of which the doctor knew nothing.

Read this story carefully, and give your imagination a test! See if you can discover what it was that the young man added to the secret message which caused the kettle to overflow with gold. Remember as you read that this is not a story from *Arabian Nights*. Here you have a story of facts stranger than fiction, facts which began in the form of an **IDEA**.

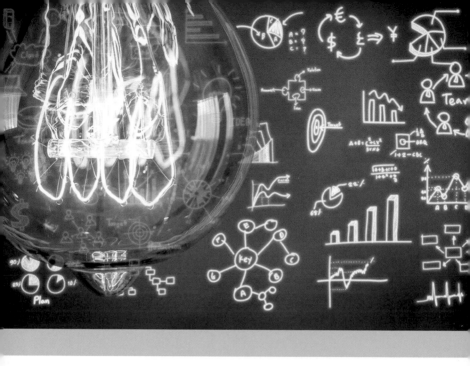

Let us take a look at the vast fortunes of gold this idea has produced. It has paid—and still pays—huge fortunes to men and women all over the world who distribute the contents of the kettle to millions of people.

The old kettle is now one of the world's largest consumers of sugar, thus providing jobs of a permanent nature to thousands of men and women engaged in growing sugar cane and in refining and marketing sugar.

The old kettle consumes, annually, millions of glass bottles, providing jobs to huge numbers of glass workers.

The influence of this idea now benefits every civilized country in the world, pouring out a continuous stream of gold to all who touch it.

Gold from the kettle built and maintains one of the most prominent colleges of the South [Emory University], where thousands of young people receive the training essential for success.

The old kettle has done other marvelous things…as this is the origin story of Coca-Cola.

All through the world depression, when factories, banks, and business houses were folding up and quitting by the thousands, the owner of this enchanted kettle went marching on, *giving continuous employment* to an army of men and women all over the world and paying out extra portions of gold to those who long ago *had faith in the idea.*

Whoever you are, wherever you may live, whatever occupation you may be engaged in, just remember in

the future, every time you see the words "Coca-Cola," that its vast empire of wealth and influence grew out of a single **IDEA**, and that the mysterious ingredient the drug clerk—Asa Candler—mixed with the secret formula was...**IMAGINATION**!

Truly, thoughts are things, and their scope of operation is the world itself.

What I Would Do If I Had a Million Dollars

This story proves the truth of that old saying, "Where there's a will, there's a way." It was told to me by that beloved educator and clergyman, the late Frank W. Gunsaulus, who began his preaching career in the stockyards region of South Chicago.

While Dr. Gunsaulus was going through college, he observed many defects in our educational system, defects which he believed he could correct if he were the head of a college. His *deepest desire* was to become the directing head of an educational institution in which young men and women would be taught to "learn by doing."

He made up his mind to organize a new college in which he could carry out his ideas without being handicapped by orthodox methods of education.

He needed a million dollars to put the project across! Where was he to lay his hands on so large a sum of money? That was the question that absorbed most of this ambitious young preacher's thought.

Being a philosopher as well as a preacher, Dr. Gunsaulus recognized, as do all who succeed in life, that **DEFINITENESS OF PURPOSE** is the starting point from which one must begin. He recognized, too, that definiteness of purpose takes on animation, life, and power when backed by a *burning desire* to translate that purpose into its material equivalent.

He knew all these great truths, yet he did not know where or how to lay his hands on a million dollars. The natural procedure would have been to give up and quit by saying, "Ah well, my idea is a good one, but I cannot do anything with it, because I never can procure the necessary million dollars." That is exactly what the majority of people would have said, but it is not what Dr. Gunsaulus said. What he said and what he did are so important that I now introduce him and let him speak for himself.

"One Saturday afternoon, I sat in my room thinking of ways and means of raising the money to carry out my plans. For nearly two years, I had been thinking, but I *had done nothing but think!*

"The time had come for **ACTION**!

"I made up my mind, then and there, that I would get the necessary million dollars within a week. How? I called the newspapers and announced I would preach a sermon the following morning, entitled, 'What I Would Do If I Had a Million Dollars.'

"I went to work on the sermon immediately, but I

must tell you, frankly, the task was not difficult, because I had been preparing that sermon for almost two years. The spirit back of it was a part of me!

"The next morning, I arose early, then knelt on my knees and asked that my sermon might come to the attention of someone who would supply the needed money.

"While I was praying, I again had that feeling of assurance that the money would be forthcoming. In my excitement, I walked out without my sermon and did not discover the oversight until I was in my pulpit and about ready to begin delivering it.

"It was too late to go back for my notes, and what a blessing that I couldn't go back! Instead, my own subconscious mind yielded the material I needed. When I arose to begin my sermon, I closed my eyes and spoke with all my heart and soul of my dreams. I not only talked to my audience, but I fancy I talked also to God. I told what I would do with a million dollars if that amount were placed in my hands. I described the plan I had in mind for organizing a great educational institution

The original Armour Institute of Technology Laboratory. Merged with Lewis Institute in 1940 to form the Illinois Institute of Technology, which still exists today.

where young people would learn to do practical things and at the same time develop their minds.

"When I had finished and sat down, a man slowly arose from his seat and made his way toward the pulpit. I wondered what he was going to do. He came into the pulpit, extended his hand, and said, 'Reverend, I liked your sermon. I believe you can do everything you said you would, if you had a million dollars. To prove that I believe in you and your sermon, if you will come to my office tomorrow morning, I will give you the million dollars. My name is Philip D. Armour.'"

Young Gunsaulus went to Mr. Armour's office, and the million dollars was presented to him. With the money, he founded the Armour Institute of Technology.

The necessary million dollars came as a result of an idea. Back of the idea was a *desire* which young Gunsaulus had been nursing in his mind for almost two years.

Observe this important fact...*He got the money within thirty six hours after he reached a definite decision in his own mind to get it and decided upon a definite plan for getting it.*

Observe that Asa Candler and Dr. Frank Gunsaulus had one characteristic in common. Both knew the astounding truth that *ideas can be transmuted into cash through the power of definite purpose plus definite plans.*

Ideas are intangible forces, but they have more power than the physical brains that give birth to them. They have the power to live on after the brain that creates them has returned to dust. For example, take the power of Christianity. That began with a simple idea, born in the brain of Christ. Its chief tenet was "Do unto others as you would have others do unto you." Christ has gone back to the source from whence He came, but His **IDEA** goes marching on. Someday, it may grow up and come into its own. Then it will have fulfilled Christ's deepest *desire*. The **IDEA** has been developing only two thousand years. Give it time!

SUCCESS REQUIRES NO EXPLANATIONS.
FAILURE PERMITS NO ALIBIS.

We are the masters of our fate, the captains of our souls, because we have the power to control our thoughts.

—NAPOLEON HILL

IMAGINATION AT WORK...

1. What does the workshop of your mind look like?

2. What is your workshop providing you in life?

3. If values convert to wealth, what values do you hold most dear?

4. Will these values transform your desire into a tangible reality of money?

5. How can you work to develop your imagination and succeed beyond limits?

3

PERSISTENCE

THREE

The Sustained Effort Necessary to Produce Success

PERSISTENCE IS AN ESSENTIAL FACTOR in the procedure of transmuting *desire* into its monetary equivalent. The basis of persistence is the power of will.

The majority of people are ready to throw their aims and purposes overboard and give up at the first sign of opposition or misfortune. A few carry on despite all opposition until they attain their goal. These few are the Fords, Carnegies, Rockefellers, and Edisons.

Persistence is a state of mind; therefore, it can be cultivated. Like all states of mind, persistence is based upon definite causes, among them these:

1. **DEFINITENESS OF PURPOSE.** Knowing what one wants is the first and perhaps the most important step toward the development of persistence. A strong motive forces one to surmount many difficulties.

2. **DESIRE.** It is comparatively easy to acquire and to maintain persistence in pursuing the object of intense desire.

3. **SELF-RELIANCE.** Belief in one's ability to carry out a plan encourages one to follow the plan through with persistence.

4. **DEFINITENESS OF PLANS.** Organized plans, even though they may be weak and entirely impractical, encourage persistence.

5. **ACCURATE KNOWLEDGE.** Knowing that one's plans are sound, based upon experience or observation, encourages persistence; "guessing" instead of "knowing" destroys persistence.

6. **COOPERATION.** Sympathy,

understanding, and harmonious cooperation with others tend to develop persistence.

7. **WILLPOWER**. The habit of concentrating one's thoughts upon the building of plans for the attainment of a definite purpose leads to persistence.

8. **HABIT**. Persistence is the direct result of habit. The mind absorbs and becomes a part of the daily experiences upon which it feeds. Fear, the worst of all enemies, can be effectively cured by forced repetition of acts of courage. Everyone who has seen active service in war knows this.

Take inventory of yourself, and determine in what particular ways, if any, you are lacking in this essential quality. Measure yourself courageously, point by point, and see how many of the eight factors of persistence you lack. The analysis may lead to discoveries that will give you a new grip on yourself.

Symptoms of Lack of Persistence

Here you will find the real enemies which stand between you and noteworthy achievement. Here you will find not only the "symptoms" indicating weakness of **PERSISTENCE**, but also the deeply seated subconscious causes of this weakness. Study the list carefully, and face yourself squarely *if you really wish to know who you are and what you are capable of doing.* These are the weaknesses which must be mastered by all who accumulate riches.

1. Failure to recognize and to clearly define exactly what one wants.

2. Procrastination, with or without cause. (Usually backed up with a formidable array of alibis and excuses.)

3. Lack of interest in acquiring specialized knowledge.

4. Indecision, the habit of "passing the buck"

on all occasions, instead of facing issues squarely. (Also backed by alibis.)

5. The habit of relying upon alibis instead of creating definite plans for the solution of problems.

6. Self-satisfaction. There is but little remedy for this affliction and no hope for those who suffer from it.

7. Indifference, usually reflected in one's readiness to compromise on all occasions, rather than meet opposition and fight it.

8. The habit of blaming others for one's mistakes and accepting unfavorable circumstances as being unavoidable.

9. Weakness of desire, due to neglect in the choice of motives that impel action.

10. Willingness, even eagerness, to quit at the first sign of defeat.

11. Lack of organized plans, placed in writing where they may be analyzed.

12. The habit of neglecting to move on ideas or to grasp opportunity when it presents itself.

13. The habit of compromising with poverty instead of aiming at riches. General absence of ambition to be, to do, and to own.

14. Wishing instead of willing.

15. Searching for all the shortcuts to riches, trying to get without giving a fair equivalent, usually reflected in the habit of gambling, endeavoring to drive "sharp" bargains.

16. Fear of criticism, failure to create plans and to put them into action because of what other people will think, do, or say. This enemy belongs at the head of the list, because it generally exists in one's subconscious mind, where its presence is not recognized.

Let us examine some of the symptoms of the fear of criticism. The majority of people permit relatives, friends, and the public at large to so influence them that they cannot live their own lives, because they fear criticism.

Huge numbers of people make mistakes in marriage, stand by the bargain, and go through life miserable and unhappy, because they fear criticism which may follow if they correct the mistake. (Anyone who has submitted to this form of fear knows the irreparable damage it does by destroying ambition, self-reliance, and the desire to achieve.)

Millions of people neglect to acquire belated education, after having left school, because they fear criticism.

Countless numbers of men and women, both young and old, permit relatives to wreck their lives in the name of duty, because they fear criticism. (Duty does not require any person to submit to the destruction of his personal ambitions and the right to live his own life in his own way.)

People refuse to take chances in business, because they fear the criticism which may follow if they fail. *The fear of criticism in such cases is stronger than the desire for success.*

Too many people refuse to set high goals for themselves or even neglect to select a career, because they fear the criticism of relatives and "friends" who may say, "Don't aim so high. People will think you are crazy."

The only breakthrough anyone can afford to rely upon is a self-made break. These come through the application of **PERSISTENCE**. The starting point is **DEFINITENESS OF PURPOSE**.

Examine the first hundred people you meet. Ask them what they want most in life, and ninety-eight of them will not be able to tell you. If you press them for an answer, some will say security, many will say money, a few will say happiness, others will say fame and power, and still others will say social recognition, ease in living, ability to sing, dance, or write, but none of them will be able to define these terms or give the slightest indication of a **PLAN** by which they hope to attain these vaguely expressed wishes. *Riches do not respond to wishes.* They respond only to definite plans, backed by definite desires through constant **PERSISTENCE**.

How to Develop Persistence

There are four simple steps which lead to the habit of **PERSISTENCE**. They call for no great amount of intelligence, no particular amount of education, and but little time or effort. The necessary steps are:

1. **A definite purpose backed by burning desire for its fulfillment.**

2. **A definite plan, expressed in continuous action.**

3. **A mind closed tightly against all negative and discouraging influences, including negative suggestions of relatives, friends, and acquaintances.**

4. **A friendly alliance with one or more persons who will encourage one to follow through with both plan and purpose.**

These four steps are essential for success in all walks of life. The entire purpose of the principles of this philosophy is to enable one to take these four steps as a matter of *habit*.

These are the steps by which one may control one's economic destiny.

They are the steps that lead to freedom and independence of thought.

They are the steps that lead to riches, in small or great quantities.

They lead the way to power, fame, and worldly recognition.

They are the four steps which guarantee favorable breaks.

They are the steps that convert dreams into physical realities.

They lead, also, to the mastery of **FEAR**, **DISCOURAGEMENT**, and **INDIFFERENCE**.

There is a magnificent reward for all who learn to take these four steps. It is the privilege of writing one's own ticket and of making life yield whatever price is asked.

Most people have achieved their greatest success just one step beyond their greatest failure.

—NAPOLEON HILL

PERSISTENCE AT WORK...

1. **How can you increase your willpower and create momentum toward achieving your goals?**

2. **How do you react when faced with obstacles?**

3. **What can you do to make your negative reactions positive steps toward persistence?**

4. **When looking at the obstacles between yourself and your goals, how can you make the impossible possible?**

5. **If "every failure brings with it the seed of an equivalent benefit," what can be learned from your failures to date?**

4

POWER OF THE MASTER MIND

FOUR

The Driving Force

POWER IS ESSENTIAL FOR SUCCESS in the accumulation of riches.

Plans are inert and useless without sufficient power to translate them into action. This chapter will describe the method by which an individual may attain and apply power.

Power may be defined as "organized and intelligently directed knowledge." Power, as the term is here used, refers to organized effort sufficient to enable an individual to transmute *desire* into its monetary equivalent. Organized effort is produced through the coordination of effort of two or more people who work toward a definite end in a spirit of harmony.

Power is required for the accumulation of money!

Power is necessary for the retention of money after it has been accumulated!

Let us ascertain how power may be acquired. If power is "organized knowledge," let us examine the sources of knowledge:

1. **INFINITE INTELLIGENCE. This source of knowledge may be contacted through faith and concentration, with the aid of creative imagination.**

2. **ACCUMULATED EXPERIENCE. The accumulated experience of man (or that portion of it which has been organized and recorded) may be found in any well-equipped public library. An important part of this accumulated experience is taught in public schools and colleges, where it has been classified and organized.**

3. **EXPERIMENT AND RESEARCH. In the field of science and in practically every**

other walk of life, men are gathering, classifying, and organizing new facts daily. This is the source to which one must turn when knowledge is not available through "accumulated experience." Here, too, the creative imagination must often be used.

Knowledge may be acquired from any of the foregoing sources. It may be converted into **POWER** by organizing it into definite **PLANS** and by expressing those plans in terms of **ACTION**.

Examination of the three major sources of knowledge will readily disclose the difficulty an individual would have if he depended upon his efforts alone in assembling knowledge and expressing it through definite plans in terms of **ACTION**. If his plans are comprehensive, and if they contemplate large proportions, he must, generally, induce others to cooperate with him before he can inject into them the necessary element of **POWER**.

Gaining Power through the Master Mind

The "Master Mind" may be defined as "coordination of knowledge and effort, in a spirit of harmony, between two or more people, for the attainment of a definite purpose."

The Master Mind principle was first called to my attention by Andrew Carnegie over twenty-five years ago. Discovery of this principle was responsible for the choice of my life's work.

Mr. Carnegie's Master Mind group consisted of a staff of approximately fifty men with whom he surrounded himself for the **DEFINITE PURPOSE** of manufacturing and marketing steel. He attributed his entire fortune to the **POWER** he accumulated through this Master Mind.

Analyze the record of any man who has accumulated a great fortune—and many of those who have accumulated modest fortunes—and you will find that they have either consciously or unconsciously employed the Master Mind principle.

Great power can be accumulated through no other principle!

It is a well-known fact that a group of electric batteries will provide more energy than a single battery. It is also a well-known fact that an individual battery will provide energy in proportion to the number and capacity of the cells it contains.

The brain functions in a similar fashion. This accounts for the fact that some brains are more efficient than

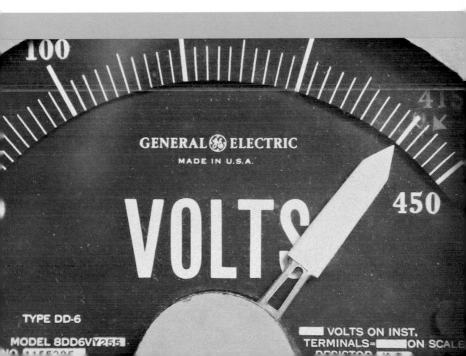

Thomas Edison, John Burroughs, and Henry Ford (circa 1914).

others and leads to this significant statement: A group of brains coordinated (or connected) in a spirit of harmony will provide more thought energy than a single brain, just as a group of electric batteries will provide more energy than a single battery.

Through this metaphor, it becomes immediately obvious that the Master Mind principle holds the secret of the power wielded by men who surround themselves with other men of brains.

There follows now another statement which will lead still nearer to an understanding of the Master Mind principle: When a group of individual brains are coordinated and function in harmony, the increased energy created through that alliance becomes available to every individual brain in the group.

It is a well-known fact that Henry Ford began his business career under the handicap of poverty, illiteracy, and ignorance. It is an equally well-known fact that within the inconceivably short period of ten years, Mr. Ford mastered these three handicaps, and that within twenty-five years, he made himself one of the richest men in America. Connect with this fact the additional knowledge that Mr. Ford's most rapid strides became noticeable from the time he became a personal friend of Thomas A. Edison, and you will begin to understand what the influence of one mind upon another can accomplish. Go a step further, and consider the fact that Mr. Ford's most outstanding achievements began from the time that he formed the acquaintances of Harvey Firestone, John Burroughs, and Luther Burbank (each a man of great brain capacity), and you will have further evidence that power may be produced through the friendly alliance of minds.

There is little if any doubt that Henry Ford is one of the best-informed men in the business and industrial world. The question of his wealth needs no discussion. Analyze Mr. Ford's intimate personal friends, some of whom have already been mentioned, and you will be prepared to understand the following statement:

"Men take on the nature and the habits and the power of thought of those with whom they associate in a spirit of sympathy and harmony."

Henry Ford whipped poverty, illiteracy, and ignorance by allying himself with great minds whose vibrations of thought he absorbed into his own mind. Through his association with Edison, Burbank, Burroughs, and Firestone, Mr. Ford added to his own brain power the sum and substance of the intelligence, experience, knowledge, and spiritual forces of these four men. Moreover, he appropriated and made use of the Master Mind principle through the methods of procedure described in this book.

This principle is available to you!

1921 Model T Ford polished to a mirror-like finish in Washington, DC (circa 1938).

Men take on the nature and the habits and the power of thought of those with whom they associate in a spirit of sympathy and harmony.

Consider the accomplishments of Mahatma Gandhi. Perhaps the majority of those who have heard of Gandhi look upon him as merely an eccentric little man who goes around without formal wearing apparel and makes trouble for the British government.

In reality, Gandhi is not eccentric, but he is the most powerful man now living. (Estimated by the number of his followers and their faith in their leader.) Moreover, he is probably the most powerful man who has ever lived. His power is passive, but it is real.

Let us study the method by which he attained his

stupendous power. It may be explained in a few words. He came by power through inducing over two hundred million people to coordinate with mind and body in a spirit of harmony for a definite purpose.

In brief, Gandhi has accomplished a miracle, for it is a miracle when two hundred million people can be induced—not forced—to cooperate in a spirit of harmony for a limitless time. If you doubt that this is a miracle, try to induce any two people to cooperate in a spirit of harmony for *any length of time*.

Every man who manages a business knows what a difficult matter it is to get employees to work together in a spirit even remotely resembling harmony.

The list of the chief sources from which power may be attained is, as you have seen, headed by infinite intelligence. When two or more people coordinate in a spirit of harmony and work toward a definite objective, they place themselves in position, through that alliance, to absorb power directly from the great universal storehouse of infinite intelligence. This is the greatest of all sources of power. It is the source to which the genius turns. It is the source to which every great leader turns (whether he may be conscious of the fact or not).

The other two major sources from which the knowledge necessary for the accumulation of power may be obtained are no more reliable than the five senses of man. The senses are not always reliable. Infinite intelligence does not err.

Money is as shy and elusive as the "old-time" maiden. It must be wooed and won by methods not unlike those used by a determined lover in pursuit of the girl of his choice. And coincidental as it is, the power used in the "wooing" of money is not greatly different than that used in wooing a maiden. That power, when successfully used in the pursuit of money, must be mixed with faith. It must be mixed with *desire*. It must be mixed with persistence. It must be applied through a plan, and that plan must be set into action.

When money comes in quantities known as "the big money," it flows to the one who accumulates it as easily

as water flows downhill. There exists a great unseen stream of power, which may be compared to a river, except that one side flows in one direction, carrying all who get into that side of the stream onward and upward to wealth, and the other side flows in the opposite direction, carrying all who are unfortunate enough to get into it (and not able to extricate themselves from it) downward to misery and poverty.

Every man who has accumulated a great fortune has recognized the existence of this stream of life. It consists of one's thinking process. The positive emotions of thought form the side of the stream which carries one to fortune. The negative emotions form the side which carries one down to poverty.

Poverty and riches often change places. The stock market crash of 1929 taught the world this truth, although the world will not long remember the lesson. Poverty may, and generally does, voluntarily take the place of riches. When riches take the place of poverty, the change is usually brought about through well-conceived and carefully executed plans. Poverty needs no plan. It needs no one to aid it, because it is bold and ruthless. Riches are shy and timid. They have to be "attracted."

Anybody can wish for riches, and most people do, but only a few know that a definite plan, plus a *burning desire* for wealth, are the only dependable means of accumulating wealth.

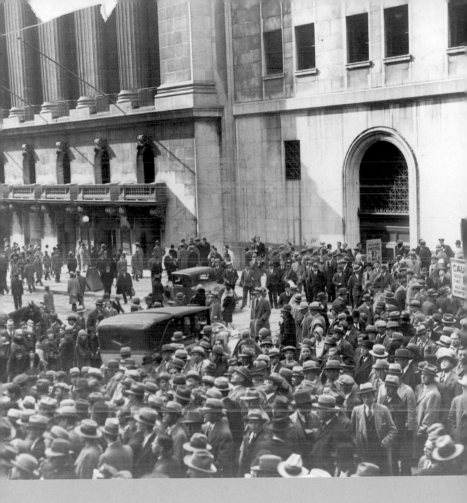

Crowd of people gathers outside the New
York Stock Exchange following the Crash
of 1929.

The ladder of success is never crowded at the top.

—NAPOLEON HILL

THE MASTER MIND AT WORK...

1. As the best plans are useless until power is used to translate them into action, how can you take action for your goals?

2. How can you tap into your own power and take these actions?

3. Knowing what results when two or more people combine their knowledge, who can you collaborate with?

4. Understanding the relationship between positive emotions and the accumulation of money, what negative emotions are holding you from riches and success?

5. How can you create more positive emotions in order to succeed?

5

GHOSTS
OF FEAR

FIVE

How to Outwit the Six
Ghosts of Fear

THE PURPOSE OF THIS CHAPTER is to turn the spotlight of attention upon the cause and the cure of the six basic fears. Before we can master an enemy, we must know its name, its habits, and its place of abode. As you read, analyze yourself carefully, and determine which, if any, of the six common fears have attached themselves to you.

The Six Basic Fears

There are six basic fears, some combination of which every human suffers at one time or another. Most people are fortunate if they do not suffer from the entire six. Named in the order of their most common appearance, they are:

The fear of **POVERTY**

The fear of **CRITICISM**

The fear of **ILL HEALTH**

The fear of **LOSS OF LOVE OF SOMEONE**

The fear of **OLD AGE**

The fear of **DEATH**

All other fears are of minor importance; they can be grouped under these six headings.

THE FEAR OF POVERTY

There can be no compromise between poverty and riches! The two roads that lead to poverty and riches travel in opposite directions. If you want riches, you must refuse to accept any circumstance that leads toward poverty. (The word "riches" is here used in its broadest sense, meaning financial, spiritual, mental, and material estates.) The starting point of the path that leads to riches is *desire*. In chapter one, you received full instructions for the proper use of *desire*. In this chapter on

FEAR, you have complete instructions for preparing your mind to make practical use of *desire*.

The fear of poverty is, without doubt, the most destructive of the six basic fears. It has been placed at the head of the list because it is the most difficult to master. Considerable courage is required to state the truth about the origin of this fear and still greater courage to accept the truth after it has been stated. The fear of poverty grew out of man's inherent tendency to *prey upon his fellow man economically*. Nearly all animals lower than man are motivated by instinct, but their capacity to "think" is limited. Therefore, they prey upon one another physically. Man, with his superior sense of intuition, with the capacity to think and to reason, does not eat his fellow man bodily. He gets more satisfaction out of "eating" him **FINANCIALLY**. Man is so avaricious that every conceivable law has been passed to safeguard him from his fellow man.

Man's obsession with money, and the hardships

that come with the lack of it, explain why the fear of poverty is atop the list.

THE FEAR OF CRITICISM

Just how man originally came by this fear, no one can state definitely, but one thing is certain—he has it in a highly developed form. Some believe that this fear made its appearance about the time that politics became a "profession."

The fear of criticism robs man of his initiative, destroys his power of imagination, limits his individuality, takes away his self-reliance, and does him damage in a hundred other ways. Parents often do their children irreparable injury by criticizing them. The mother of one of my boyhood chums used to punish him with a switch almost daily, always completing the job with the statement, "You'll land in the penitentiary before you are twenty." He was sent to a reformatory at the age of seventeen.

Criticism is the one form of service of which everyone

has too much. Everyone has a stock of it which is handed out, gratis, whether called for or not. One's nearest relatives often are the worst offenders. It should be recognized as a crime (in reality, it is a crime of the worst nature) for any parent to build inferiority complexes in the mind of a child through unnecessary criticism. Employers who understand human nature get the best there is in men not by criticism but by constructive suggestion. Parents may accomplish the same results with their children. Criticism will plant **FEAR** in the human heart, or resentment, but it will not build love or affection.

THE FEAR OF ILL HEALTH

This fear may be traced to both physical and social heredity. It is closely associated, as to its origin, with the causes of fear of old age and the fear of death, because it leads one closely to the border of "terrible worlds" of which man knows not but concerning which he has been taught some discomforting stories. The opinion is somewhat general, also, that certain unethical people engaged in the business of "selling health" have had not a little to do with keeping alive the fear of ill health.

Doctors send patients into new climates for their health, because a change of "mental attitude" is necessary. The seed of fear of ill health lives in every human mind. Worry, fear, discouragement, and disappointment in love and business affairs cause this seed to germinate and grow. The recent business depression kept the doctors on the run, because every form of negative thinking may cause ill health.

Disappointments in business and in love stand at the head of the list of causes of fear of ill health. A young man suffered a disappointment in love which sent him to a hospital. For months, he hovered between life and death. A specialist in suggestive therapeutics was called in. The specialist changed nurses, placing him in the charge of a very *charming young woman* who began (by prearrangement with the doctor) to pretend affection for him the first day of her arrival on the job. Within three weeks, the patient was discharged from the hospital,

still suffering, but with an entirely different malady. **HE WAS IN LOVE AGAIN**. The remedy began as a hoax, but the patient and the nurse were later married.

THE FEAR OF LOSS OF LOVE

Jealousy grows out of man's inherited fear of the loss of love of someone. This fear is the most painful of all the six basic fears. It probably plays more havoc with the body and mind than any of the other basic fears, as it often leads to permanent insanity.

The fear of the loss of love probably dates back to

the Stone Age, when men stole women by brute force. They continue to steal women, but their technique has changed. Instead of force, they now use persuasion, the promise of pretty clothes, motorcars, and other "bait" much more effective than physical force. Man's habits are the same as they were at the dawn of civilization, but he expresses them differently.

Careful analysis has shown that women are just as susceptible to this fear as men. This fact is also easily explained. Women have learned, from experience, that men are polygamous by nature, that they are not to be trusted in the hands of rivals.

THE FEAR OF OLD AGE

In the main, this fear grows out of two sources. First, the thought that old age may bring with it poverty when one can no longer work. Secondly, and by far the most common source of origin, from false and cruel teachings of the past which have been too well mixed with fire and brimstone and other bogeys cunningly designed to enslave man through fear.

In the basic fear of old age, man has two very sound reasons for his apprehension—one growing out of his distrust of his fellow man, who may seize whatever worldly goods he may possess, and the other arising from the terrible pictures of the world beyond, which were planted in his mind through social heredity before he came into full possession of his mind.

The possibility of ill health, which is more common as people grow older, is also a contributing cause of this common fear of old age. Eroticism also enters into the cause of the fear of old age, as no man cherishes the thought of diminishing sex attraction.

The most common cause of fear of old age is associated with the possibility of poverty. "Poorhouse" is not a pretty word. It throws a chill into the mind of every person who faces the possibility of having to spend his declining years on a poor farm.

Another contributing cause of the fear of old age is the possibility of loss of freedom and independence, as old age may bring with it the loss of both physical and economic freedom.

THE FEAR OF DEATH

To some, this is the cruelest of all the basic fears. The reason is obvious. The terrible pangs of fear associated with the thought of death, in the majority of cases, may be charged directly to religious fanaticism. So-called heathens are less afraid of death than the more "civilized." For hundreds of millions of years, man has been asking the still-unanswered questions "whence" and "whither." Where did I come from, and where am I going?

In truth, **NO MAN KNOWS**, and no man has ever

known, what heaven or hell is like, nor does any man know if either place actually exists. This very lack of positive knowledge opens the door of the human mind to the charlatan so he may enter and control that mind with his stock of legerdemain and various brands of pious fraud and trickery.

This fear is useless. Death will come, no matter what anyone may think about it. Accept it as a necessity, and pass the thought out of your mind. It must be a necessity, or it would not come to all. Perhaps it is not as bad as it has been pictured.

The entire world is made up of only two things, *energy* and *matter*. In elementary physics, we learn that neither matter nor energy (the only two realities known to man) can be created nor destroyed. Both matter and energy can be transformed, but neither can be destroyed.

Life is energy, if it is anything. If neither energy nor matter can be destroyed, of course life cannot be destroyed. Life, like other forms of energy, may be passed through various processes of transition or change, but it cannot be destroyed. Death is mere transition.

If death is not mere change or transition, then nothing comes after death except a long, eternal, peaceful sleep, and sleep is nothing to be feared. Thus you may wipe out, forever, the fear of death.

Worry

Worry is a state of mind based upon fear. It works slowly but persistently. It is insidious and subtle. Step by step, it digs itself in until it paralyzes one's reasoning faculty, destroys self-confidence and initiative. Worry is a form of sustained fear caused by indecision; therefore it is a state of mind which can be controlled.

Kill the habit of worry in all its forms by reaching a general blanket decision that *nothing which life has to offer is worth the price of worry*. With this decision will come poise, peace of mind, and calmness of thought, which will bring happiness.

A man whose mind is filled with fear not only destroys his own chances of intelligent action, but transmits these destructive vibrations to the minds of all who come into contact with him and also destroys their chances.

Your business in life is presumably to achieve success. To be successful, you must find peace of mind, acquire the material needs of life, and, above all, attain **HAPPINESS**. All of these evidences of success begin in the form of thought impulses.

You may control your own mind; you have the power to feed it whatever thought impulses you choose. With this privilege comes the responsibility of using it constructively. You are the master of your own earthly destiny just as surely as you have the power to control your own thoughts. You may influence, direct, and eventually control your own environment, making your life what you want it to be—or you may neglect to exercise the privilege which is yours, to make your life to order, thus casting yourself upon the broad sea of circumstance where you will be tossed hither and yon like a chip on the waves of the ocean.

The Seventh Basic Evil

In addition to the six basic fears, there is another evil by which people suffer. It constitutes a rich soil in which the seeds of failure grow abundantly. It is so subtle that its presence often is not detected. For want of a better name, let us call this evil **SUSCEPTIBILITY TO NEGATIVE INFLUENCES**.

You can easily protect yourself against highway robbers, because the law provides organized cooperation for your benefit, but the "seventh basic evil" is more difficult to master, because it strikes when you are not aware of its presence—when you are asleep, and while you are awake. Moreover, its weapon is intangible, because it consists of merely a **STATE OF MIND**. This evil is also dangerous because it strikes in as many different forms as there are human experiences. Sometimes, it enters the mind through the well-meant words of one's own relatives. At other times, it bores from within, through one's own mental attitude. Always, it is as deadly as poison, even though it may not kill as quickly.

How to Protect Yourself against Negative Influences

To protect yourself against negative influences, whether of your own making or the result of the activities of negative people around you, recognize that you have **WILLPOWER** and put it into constant use until it builds a wall of immunity against negative influences in your own mind.

Recognize the fact that you and every other human being is by nature lazy, indifferent, and susceptible to all suggestions which harmonize with your weaknesses.

Recognize that you are, by nature, susceptible to all the six basic fears, and set up habits for the purpose of counteracting all these fears.

Recognize that negative influences often work on you through your subconscious mind, therefore they are difficult to detect, and keep your mind closed against all people who depress or discourage you in any way.

Clean out your medicine chest, throw away all pill bottles, and stop pandering to colds, aches, pains, and imaginary illness.

Deliberately seek the company of people who influence you to THINK AND ACT FOR YOURSELF.

Do not ACCEPT troubles as they have a tendency not to disappoint.

Without doubt, the most common weakness of all human beings is the habit of leaving their minds open to the negative influence of other people. This weakness is all the more damaging, because most people do not recognize that they are cursed by it, and many who acknowledge it neglect or refuse to correct the evil until it becomes an uncontrollable part of their daily habits.

You have **ABSOLUTE CONTROL** over but one thing, and that is your thoughts. This is the most significant and inspiring of all facts known to man! It reflects man's divine nature. This divine prerogative is the sole means by which you may control your own destiny. If you fail to control your own mind, you may be sure you will control nothing else.

Mind control is the result of self-discipline and habit. You either control your mind or it controls you. There is no halfway compromise. The most practical of all methods for controlling the mind is the habit of keeping it busy with a definite purpose, backed by a definite plan. Study the record of any man who achieves noteworthy success, and you will observe that he has control over his own mind, moreover that he exercises that control and directs it toward the attainment of definite objectives. Without this control, success is not possible.

Famous Alibis

People who do not succeed have one distinguishing trait in common. They know *all the reasons for failure* and have what they believe to be airtight alibis to explain away their own lack of achievement.

Some of these alibis are clever, and a few of them are justifiable by the facts. But alibis cannot be used for money. The world wants to know only one thing: **HAVE YOU ACHIEVED SUCCESS**?

A character analyst compiled a list of the most commonly used alibis. As you read the list, examine yourself carefully, and determine how many of these alibis, if any, are your own property. Remember, too, the philosophy presented in this book makes *every one* of these alibis obsolete.

IF I had money...

IF I had a good education...

IF I could get a job...

IF I had good health...

IF I only had time...

IF times were better...

IF other people understood me...

IF I could meet "the right people"...

IF I had the talent that some people have...

IF I were only free...

IF I had the personality of some people...

IF I were attractive...

IF people weren't so dumb...

IF I had the courage to see myself as I really am...

The only alibi that truly matters is the last one. If we could all have courage and believe in ourselves, we could create the life we are dreaming of. To take this thought to its natural conclusion... "If I had the courage to see myself as I really am, I would *find out what is wrong with me and correct it.* Then I might have a chance to profit by my mistakes and learn something from the experience of others, for I know that there is something **WRONG** with me, or I would now be where **I WOULD HAVE BEEN IF** I had spent more time analyzing my weaknesses and less time building alibis to cover them."

Building alibis with which to explain away failure is a national pastime. The habit is as old as the human race and is *fatal to success*! Why do people cling to their pet alibis? The answer is obvious. They defend their alibis because they create them! A man's alibi is the child of his own imagination. It is human nature to defend one's own brainchild.

Building alibis is a deeply rooted habit. Habits are difficult to break, especially when they provide justification for something we do. However, as with all the principles outlined within, the reward is worthy of your effort. Will you make the start and be convinced?

Life is a checkerboard, and the player opposite you is TIME. If you hesitate before moving or neglect to move promptly, your men will be wiped off the board by TIME. You are playing against a partner who will not tolerate INDECISION!

—NAPOLEON HILL

All achievements, all earned riches have their beginning in an idea."

—NAPOLEON HILL

THE GHOSTS OF FEAR AT WORK...

1. Which of the ghosts of fear most threatens to defeat any desire or plan you may have?

2. How can you defeat your personal ghosts of fear to have successful use of your mind?

3. Recognizing that indecision is the seedling of fear, how can you confidently move forward in your choices?

4. How can you have the necessary control over your state of mind?

5. Realizing that both riches and poverty are a state of mind, how do you define success and failure? How can you make your perpetual mental state one of success?

ABOUT NAPOLEON HILL
AND THE NAPOLEON HILL FOUNDATION

Oliver Napoleon Hill was an American self-help author. He is best known for his original release of the book *Think and Grow Rich* (1937) which is among the ten bestselling self-help books of all time. Napoleon Hill died at age eighty-seven on November 8, 1970. He had just celebrated his birthday on October 26. Despite the urban legend, he did not die penniless. He had endowed his foundation and was living his dream. You can read his biography—*Lifetime of Riches*—to learn more about his family and later years.

Working in his name, the Napoleon Hill Foundation is a nonprofit educational institution dedicated to making the world a better place in which to live.